THE BEGINNINGS OF FARMING

The early Egyptians learned how to grow crops. The annual flooding of the river valleys where the first civilizations were set up, left a rich silt on the land. This happened with the Nile, allowing the Egyptians to farm their valley.

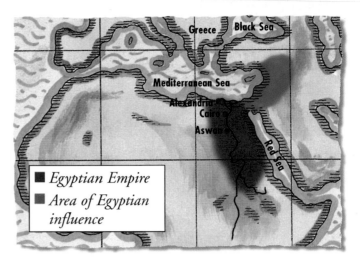

- ■ *Egyptian Empire*
- ■ *Area of Egyptian influence*

A KINGDOM UNITED

Originally, Egypt was divided into two kingdoms, Upper and Lower Egypt. They were united under Pharaoh Menes in c.3100 BCE, who founded the 1st Dynasty. The Old Kingdom lasted from the 3rd to the 6th dynasty, following an intermediate period the Middle Kingdom lasted from the 11th to 12th dynasty. The New Kingdom period (c.1550–1070 BCE) saw great military expansion.

MONUMENTAL BUILDINGS

The Egyptians built pyramids to house the bodies of their dead kings (pharaohs). The king was buried with precious goods to take on his journey into the afterlife. The Great Pyramid of Khufu (Cheops) at Giza (shown above) was built in c.2551 BCE.

SIGN OF LIFE

This dish, in the form of an ankh cross, was used for offerings to the gods. It was only carried by the king or queen. The ankh was the Egyptian symbol for life.

THE FIRST WRITING

The first known system of writing appeared in Sumeria, north-east of Egypt, around 3200 BCE, in the form of simple pictograms. The Egyptians developed this into an incredibly complex system of writing called hieroglyphs, using over 700 different symbols. The symbols expressed ideas, rather than words, and were used mainly for sacred writings.

ORNATE FURNITURE

Wood was in short supply in Egypt, but the wealthy could afford exotic imports. Carpenters were skilled craftsmen and decorated their work with fine inlays and friezes, as seen in this chair.

LIFE FOR THE RICH

Because it all happened so long ago, it is difficult to get a complete picture of everyday life in ancient Egypt. The remains we have are the belongings of the wealthy and, more especially, royalty. The wonderful buildings, art and artefacts tell us about their skills and wealth. The hieroglyphs and scripts are about government and ritual. However, we know very little about what life was like for ordinary people. Comfort and hygiene were important to all Egyptians, and they had very strong family values.

ORNAMENTAL GLASS

The arts of glass-making and enamelling were well known to the Egyptians. They also made fine white and coloured porcelain of the same quality as that made in China. Houses of the wealthy were decorated with many fine art pieces, such as this beautiful glass perfume bottle in the shape of a bulti fish.

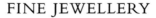

FINE JEWELLERY

Egyptian jewellery was very striking. Skilled metalworkers made all sorts of shapes by welding thin strips of metal into complicated designs using molten sulphur. Gold (beaten or moulded) and fine jewels, such as turquoise and amethyst, were commonly used. They were decorated with fine ceramics and painted glass.

KEEPING UP APPEARANCES

Most Egyptians took a pride in their appearance, especially the wealthy who could afford the finest materials. Both men and women had their hair cut short, but wore elaborately braided and decorated wigs. The wealthier they were, the more elaborate their headdresses were, such as a gold headband decorated with semi-precious stones, as seen here.

ROOMY HOUSES

The houses of the rich were quite large, often with two storeys. They were made from bricks, covered in plaster then painted white. They were built on platforms to protect against damp, as shown on this papyrus.

COMFORTABLE LIFESTYLE

Houses were quite comfortably, if simply, furnished, making great use of rare woods and fabrics imported from abroad. Most furniture was quite elaborately carved, such as lion-claw feet on tables and chairs. Beds, complete with stuffed mattresses, also had head and foot rests and sloping back boards. The wooden head rest shown here was probably used for resting during the day.

LIFE FOR THE POOR

TIMELESS SCENE

Over 90 percent of Egypt is desert. Virtually the only fertile region capable of supporting life, apart from small oases, was along the flood plains of the River Nile. Many of the farming techniques practised today have hardly changed since then.

Although life for the poor was hard in ancient Egypt, by comparison to other societies of the time, even they were quite well-off. Most peasants worked in the fields, while many others were employed in the massive building programmes of the pharaohs. Most were well treated. A good family life was important to all classes of Egyptians. Elderly relatives were highly respected. When children became teenagers, they often became servants to wealthier families. Houses, in both town and country, were built with bricks, made from mud and straw then baked in the sun.

GETTING ABOUT

Few poor people could afford wagons, horses or camels to transport themselves and their goods about. Most people used donkeys. There were few proper roads, so travelling was always difficult. For many people, the only journeys they ever made were to and from the local market. Donkeys still provide the main means of transport for poor Egyptians in remote areas today.

BASIC ACCOMMODATION

This clay model shows a typical poor Egyptian's house with an arched doorway and small windows to keep the heat out.

A MEASURE OF WEALTH

A man's wealth was measured by the number of beasts he owned, such as goats, geese and particularly cattle. Scribes recorded the details and people were then taxed. The farming season in ancient Egypt was set by the annual flooding of the Nile. Each year, the river burst its banks, leaving thick, black silt over a large area of the surrounding land, making it very fertile.

HARD LABOUR

This wall painting from the Sennudem tomb in Thebes dates from c.1200 BCE and shows farming practices at about that time. An ox is used to pull a wooden plough. The ploughman is using a whip, made from papyrus, to kill flies and drive on the ox.

SLAVE TRADE

Although the ancient Egyptians ruled over a small empire in north Africa and the eastern Mediterranean, they were not a war-like people. When they went into other lands, they captured native peoples and brought them back to Egypt as slaves. Some were put to work as servants, but mostly they were sent to work on the almost continuous building programmes of the pharaohs.

SPICE OF LIFE

Egypt was at the centre of the known world and all major trade routes passed through it, bringing exotic foods and spices from the East. Banquets could be very grand.

VINTAGE WINE

The Egyptians grew grapes both as a dessert and for making wine. Wine was usually only drunk by the rich. The more common alcoholic drink was beer, which was made from barley and was very thick.

A SWEETENER

To sweeten their foods, Egyptians used either fruits, such as dates, or honey. Bees were kept in conical pottery hives, as shown here.

FAMILY AFFAIR

This detail from a stucco wall painting comes from the tomb of Sennedjem and shows the tomb owner and his wife working in the fields. There was no centrally organized system of farming and each family produced their own food. The Egyptians are believed to have invented the first ox-drawn plough in about 3100 BCE.

FOOD AND DRINK

Most Egyptians ate very well, although they suffered from plagues of insects that destroyed their crops and caused famine. Farming methods were quite basic and most people grew just enough food for their own family. However, the people could choose from a wide range of foods, including different meats, fish, vegetables (such as onions, leeks, turnips and garlic) and fruit (including grapes, figs, dates and pomegranates). They learned how to hatch chickens' eggs so they always had a good supply of poultry. Wine, made from grapes and dates, was popular with the wealthy. However, in the 7th century CE, Egypt was taken over by the Arabs. Islam became the official religion and as Muslims do not drink alcohol, the people stopped drinking wine and beer.

THE BUTCHER'S TRADE

Wealthy Egyptians enjoyed a variety of meats, including sheep, oxen, poultry and wild animals, such as antelope, as shown here.

OPEN HEARTHS

Cooking was usually done in clay ovens or open charcoal fires, as shown here. The kitchen was often outside, away from the living rooms, to avoid the risk of fires and to reduce smells.

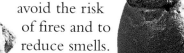

HIGH-FIBRE DIET

The Egyptian diet contained plenty of fibre, as flour used in bread-making was only coarsely ground. Bread, made from barley and wheat, was the basic diet of many Egyptians. Bakers also made a variety of cakes using fruits, such as figs.

PASTIMES

From discoveries about ancient Egypt, it appears that life was generally good for most people, especially during during the 18th and 19th dynasties (c. 1550–1196 BCE). They spent a lot of time enjoying themselves, rather than working. Poorer societies had to work hard just to provide food and shelter, but the Egyptians enjoyed their pastimes, either on their own or with their family. Unlike the Greeks and Romans, they did not take part in large-scale, public pastimes, such as going to the theatre or the stadium.

ORIGIN OF THE OLYMPICS?

Egyptians were keen on exercise. Popular sports were boxing, wrestling, gymnastics and jousting from boats, which may have led on to the Greek Olympics.

GYPSIES

Modern–day gypsies may not be descended from eastern Europeans, as is sometimes suggested, but from Egyptians who fled their homeland at the time of the Greek occupation. Many traditional gypsy pastimes, such as horse racing and singing and dancing, may also have been practised in ancient Egypt.

EXOTIC DANCERS

A popular pastime in the king's palace, or at banquets held by the rich, was song and dance. Servant girls were trained to dance and they performed, sometimes naked, with gymnasts and jugglers, while musicians played.

THE FIRST HARP

It is believed that the Egyptians invented the harp (shown left) some time around 3100 BCE. Harps varied in size from small, lyre-like examples to ones taller than a man. The hollow chamber was usually made out of wood.

SENET

This senet board is made from wood and contains a drawer to house the playing pieces. The board is divided into 30 squares and dates from about 1200 BCE.

BOARD GAMES

Board games were very popular with the Egyptians. The most popular was senet, in which two players tried to reach the kingdom of the gods. In the example left, the board has been drawn onto a papyrus sheet. Other games, still played today, were backgammon and chess.

FAMILY VALUES

Egyptian society, at all levels, had strong family values. Families were quite large, with between 8 and 12 children. Though children were expected to work, there was still plenty of time for play. Egyptians were great storytellers and everyone gathered round to hear the father recite tales of the gods and of heroic deeds.

HEADDRESS

It was fashionable for men and women to wear either wigs, made from human hair and held in place by beeswax, or headdresses. These might be hats made of fine material, or look like wigs, with finely braided hair and decorated with jewels. For the poorer classes, working in the fierce Egyptian sun, skull caps or bonnets were worn.

FASHION

*A*ll Egyptians liked to wear brightly painted make-up or jewellery. Personal appearance was very important to them and they were also very fashion-conscious. Egypt was at the centre of most of the trade routes to the Mediterranean and the East and new materials brought back from countries, such as India, were quickly bought up. Because of the hot climate, most clothes were simple, light and loose fitting. Men usually wore only a kilt or loin cloth. Women wore skirts or dresses, similar to ~~Indian~~ saris.

HAIRSTYLES

Most men and women had their hair cut short. They preferred wigs, or hair extensions fastened with hair pins made of wood or bone. Fine-toothed combs made of wood or, as shown here, ivory, were used to create elaborate hairstyles on the wigs.

FOOTWEAR

This picture shows the production of papyrus, used to make a wide range of objects, including shoes. Occasionally, shoes were made of leather, but most footwear consisted of simple sandals made from papyrus reeds. They were cheap to make and easily replaced.

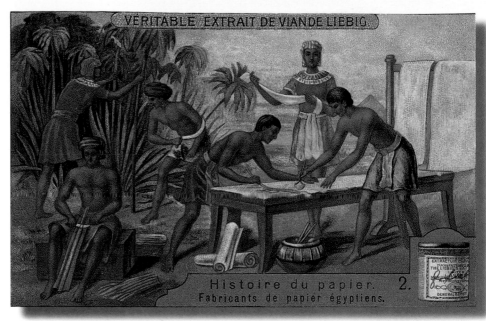

VÉRITABLE EXTRAIT DE VIANDE LIEBIG

Histoire du papier. 2.
Fabricants de papier égyptiens.

BODY BEAUTIFUL

Make-up was widely used and held in elaborately carved containers, such as shown above. Various minerals (some poisonous) were ground up to form pastes. Green eye shadow, made from malachite, was a favourite.

ADORNMENTS

Poorer people wore jewellery, such as rings and bracelets, made of cheap metals and brightly painted clay. The wealthy used gold and precious stones, available from the East. This gold and lapis lazuli necklace (left) and scarab pectoral (right) came from the tomb of Tutankhamun.

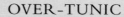

OVER-TUNIC

Women usually wore long, loose-fitting dresses, often made out of one piece of material and pleated. The over-tunic shown here is believed to be the oldest surviving garment in the world and dates from about 3000 BCE.

ART AND ARCHITECHURE

MONUMENTAL ART

Most of the important works of art and architecture that have survived are from temples and tombs. Built on a grand scale, they do not tell us about ancient Egyptian society as a whole. Building on this scale was never attempted again, not even in classical Greece and Rome. This view shows King Ramesses the Great at Luxor.

One of the most amazing things about the remains of ancient Egypt is the huge size of its monuments. However, many of the larger buildings were not actually built, but were carved out of solid rock. The Sphynx at Giza, for example, was made in this way, as well as many statues and entrances to the great temples. Even the Great Pyramid contains an enormous mound of natural bedrock at its centre. A lot of knowledge about everyday life in ancient Egypt comes from the engravings and reliefs on temple walls and pillars. The Egyptians created many fine works of art, including wall paintings, statues, pottery and jewellery. They saw these as part of life itself and not separate from their day-to-day lives.

BUILDING THE PYRAMIDS

To build the pyramids, large blocks of stone were dragged across the desert. After the first level of blocks was in place, workers built ramps of mudbrick, limestone chips and clay. Large stones were dragged up the ramps to build the next level. Building took around 20 years to finish.

TEMPLE OF ABU SIMBEL

Rameses II revived the colossal style of architectural building that had gone out of fashion. He built many huge statues of himself. At Abu Simbel, in the Upper Nile, he built a grand temple of himself and three gods.

OBELISKS

Obelisks are tall, squared monoliths with pointed tops. They were usually placed in pairs at the entrance to temples. Hieroglyphs carved on their sides showed who built them and to which god they were dedicated. This one, along with the colossal statues of Rameses II can be seen at Luxor.

TEMPLE OF KARNAK

The Egyptians never managed to build using arches. Instead, they roofed their buildings with huge flat slabs or corbelling, a series of slabs, each built out from the one below in decreasing steps until the gap was closed. This view above shows the temple at Karnak, built by Ramesses II.

THE PYRAMIDS OF GIZA

The great pyramids of Giza were built as tombs for Egyptian pharaohs. The Great Pyramid (right) was built around 2551 BCE for King Khufu. His mummified body was entombed in a secret chamber to protect it against grave robbers, along with treasures for him to take into the afterlife. Despite hidden entrances and blocked-off passageways, Khufu's tomb was still looted and the robber's tunnel is now the main entrance. It is 146.6 metres high, contains about 2,300,000 blocks of stone.

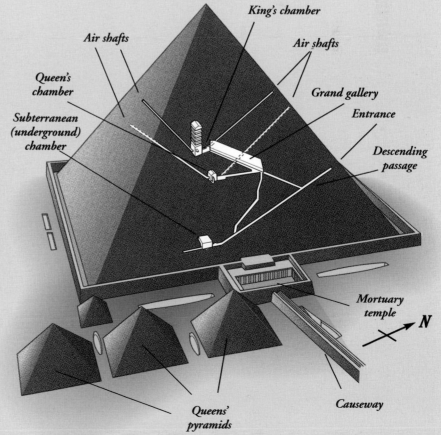

King's chamber

Air shafts

Air shafts

Queen's chamber

Grand gallery

Subterranean (underground) chamber

Entrance

Descending passage

Mortuary temple

N

Queens' pyramids

Causeway

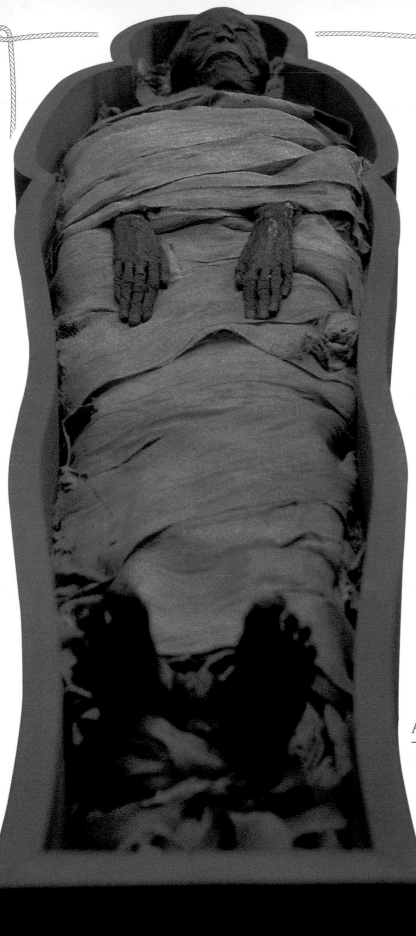

EMBALMING

Embalmers understood the causes of decay in bodies and so removed all of the internal organs. They even removed the brain through the nostrils!

DOCTOR PRIESTS

In the early years of their civilization, the Egyptians thought disease was caused by an invasion of the body by evil spirits. Until physicians were allowed to practise medicine, only priests could cure the sick.

ANATOMY

Because Egyptians believed in an afterlife, doctors could not study human corpses. They had to rely on the examination of animals for their understanding of anatomy (the structure of the body).

HEALTH AND MEDICINE

*T*he ancient Egyptians had good medical skills and they knew about human anatomy. However, medical treatment was a mixture of science and magic. Many illnesses were thought to be caused by worm-like creatures in the body, which needed to be removed from the sick person. The herbal cures that the Egyptians used, such as garlic, are still in use in natural medicine today. Magical charms (amulets) were worn to protect people from disease, and they made offerings and sacrifices to the gods. Because Egyptians believed in an afterlife, they buried magical charms with the body to protect it in the underworld. Life expectancy was high and many Egyptians lived to over the age of 80.

DENTISTRY

This relief comes from the tomb of Hesire, chief dentist and physician to the king, and dates from c.2700 BCE. Studies of mummified bodies have revealed quite complicated dentistry skills.

NATIONAL HEALTH

The State of Egypt paid doctors' wages, allowing them to treat people free of charge during wartime. Priests had to keep themselves free of disease, which included having their heads completely shaved, as shown here.

PURE AIR

Breathing the scent of the sacred lotus flower was thought to be a protection against disease. Egyptians knew of the healing properties of several plants, which they made into remedies.

LOVE AND MARRIAGE

LEGENDARY LOVE

Sometimes royal children were married to each other to keep ruling power in their family. In religion, the sky goddess Nut was married to her brother, the Earth god Geb, seen here.

Ordinary people in Egyptian society lived a relaxed lifestyle with plenty of time for fun and socializing. After about the age of 12, children were treated as adults and allowed to marry. Many girls married early because they only had limited work opportunities. After marriage, men were expected to provide for their family and women looked after elderly parents. Priests were highly respected in Egyptian society. They devoted their lives to the gods and pharaoh but were also allowed to marry and have families. Priests became very rich and owned a great deal of land through a system of inheritance.

GODDESS OF FERTILITY

The Egyptian goddess of fertility was Taweret, usually shown as a pregnant hippopotamus. Taweret often has a fierce expression to ward off evil during childbirth. Women said prayers and made offerings to her during pregnancy. In general, however, hippos were regarded as evil and were seen as the enemies of the gods Osiris and Horus.

FAMILY VIRTUES

The ancient Egyptians valued good behaviour. Single girls of high rank were escorted on their meetings with men, and many marriages were arranged to ensure a good match, or to secure an income or inheritance. This was especially true for women who did not have money of their own.

GIRL POWER

Ancient Egypt was a society ruled by men, although women who married important nobles could have a great deal of influence through their husbands. This couple probably stayed together all their lives. Their heavy wigs show that they were very wealthy.

DEVOTED COUPLE

Unlike other Middle-Eastern societies, ancient Egyptians were monogamous (men were only allowed one wife at a time though some of the pharaohs and nobles may have had more). Divorce was very easy for people of all classes. This *stela* (a religious inscription placed inside a tomb, like a gravestone) shows a loving couple who share the same grave.

WEDDING CEREMONY

This wall painting shows a Nubian called Sennufer marrying his bride. They are being blessed by the high priest, using a sacred container called a *situla*. Brides often wore sacred lotus blossoms in their hair for good luck.

WOMEN AND CHILDREN

Although ancient Egyptian society was ruled by men (few positions of power or authority were given to women), women played an important role in providing a stable family life. Only the wealthy could afford servants or slaves to work in the house. For most families, it was the women who looked after the house, cared for the children, cooked and cleaned. There were few good jobs for women. Most doctors and priests were men, though occasionally an upper-class woman might become a priestess.

CHILDREN'S GAMES

These carvings show children carrying models in the shape of birds. These would have floated on water in much the same way as model boats do. Many modern games can be traced back to Egyptian times, including leapfrog.

CLEOPATRA

Egypt was attacked several times from about 1000 BCE. Cleopatra VII (above), although from a Greek family, was the last ruler of Egypt. Unusually for a woman, she ruled in her own right. She had a disastrous love-affair with the Roman general, Mark Anthony, and together they attacked Rome. When their armies were defeated by Octavius in 30 CE, Cleopatra killed herself. From then on, Egypt became a Roman province.

TIME-HONOURED TRADITION

Two of the principal roles for women were to make and wash the clothes for the family. The most common material was linen. This was woven from the stems of the flax plant, making a strong and durable fabric.

QUEEN NEFERTITI

Queen Nefertiti ruled with her husband Akhenaten in the 14th century BCE. Nefertiti helped Akhenaten stop the worship of the old gods. People were made to worship a sun god – Aten – instead. This made them very unpopular, and when they died, their names were removed from many books and inscriptions. In about 1333 BCE, Tutankhamun announced that the old gods could be worshipped again.

HARVESTING

Women and children did most of the work on the farms. This woman had picked fruit, carrying her child in a papoose.

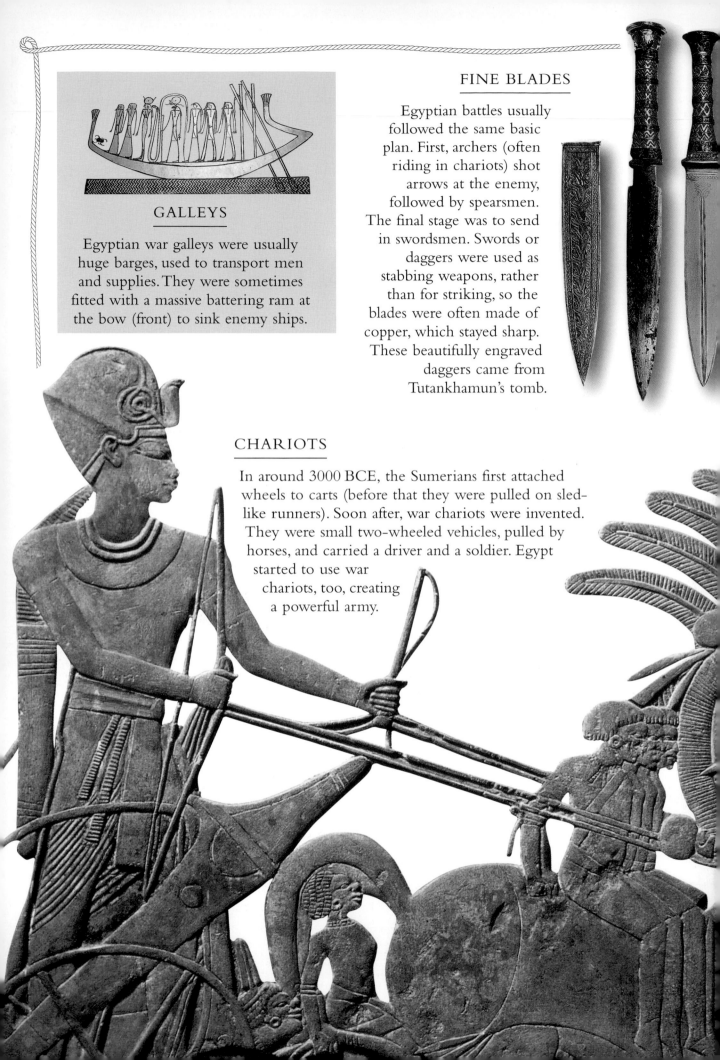

GALLEYS

Egyptian war galleys were usually huge barges, used to transport men and supplies. They were sometimes fitted with a massive battering ram at the bow (front) to sink enemy ships.

FINE BLADES

Egyptian battles usually followed the same basic plan. First, archers (often riding in chariots) shot arrows at the enemy, followed by spearsmen. The final stage was to send in swordsmen. Swords or daggers were used as stabbing weapons, rather than for striking, so the blades were often made of copper, which stayed sharp. These beautifully engraved daggers came from Tutankhamun's tomb.

CHARIOTS

In around 3000 BCE, the Sumerians first attached wheels to carts (before that they were pulled on sled-like runners). Soon after, war chariots were invented. They were small two-wheeled vehicles, pulled by horses, and carried a driver and a soldier. Egypt started to use war chariots, too, creating a powerful army.

WAR AND WEAPONS

etween 5000 and 3100 BCE there were two kingdoms – Upper and Lower Egypt. In about 3100 BCE, Pharaoh Menes united the two kingdoms and founded the first dynasty. Egyptian civilization was very successful from then on. It was made up of settlements along the Nile valley. During the New Kingdom period (c.1550–1070 BCE), Egypt expanded and formed a small empire stretching from Nubia in the south, to Sumer and Syria in the north. As Egypt was a rich country, other nations tried to invade but the army was fierce in protecting its borders. Later, however, Egypt was invaded many times.

TACTICS

The army was a very organized and powerful fighting force. In battle, soldiers marched in divisions of 50 straight towards enemy lines. They often won because they outnumbered their enemies. Rameses II is seen here defeating his enemies, the Nubians, Libyans and Syrians.

WARRIORS

Favourite weapons in the Egyptian army were the spear and the battle-axe. Axes were often quite elaborate, with bronze heads. Soldiers had quite light armour, usually helmets and large wooden shields, used as protection against arrows or spears.

PROTECTION OF THE GODS

When the Egyptians went on a military campaign, they asked the gods to both protect and help them in defeating their enemies. A mast was carried on the pharaoh's chariot, decorated with a ram's head and a symbol of the sun to represent Amun-Re. Many other gods might accompany the army, including Khansu the moon god, shown here.

CRIME AND PUNISHMENT

COUNTERFEIT

Coins were introduced into Egypt in 525 BCE, when the Persians invaded. After that date anyone found guilty of making counterfeit coins had their hands cut off. The gold coin shown here is from Cleopatra's time (c.40 CE).

Ancient Egyptian laws were very strict and everyone was expected to obey them. Some of these laws were harsh, but the pharaohs believed that if the people were protected from crime, they would be happy and would give more back to society. Everyone had a duty to report crimes and to help anyone in danger. In fact, it was a crime not to! Punishments reflected the sort of the crime commited. An unfaithful wife had her nose cut off so she was no longer beautiful. Forgers who made counterfeit coins had their hands cut off. Anyone found guilty of treason (betraying Egypt) had their tongue removed.

ALL-SEEING GOD

The pharaoh was thought to be the human form of the hawk-headed sky god, Horus. He was an all-seeing god who ensured that every citizen was protected. If a guilty person escaped punishment in life, they might still pay the price in death. If they were justly accused of a crime, even after death, they might not be allowed burial honours, so they could not enter the afterlife.

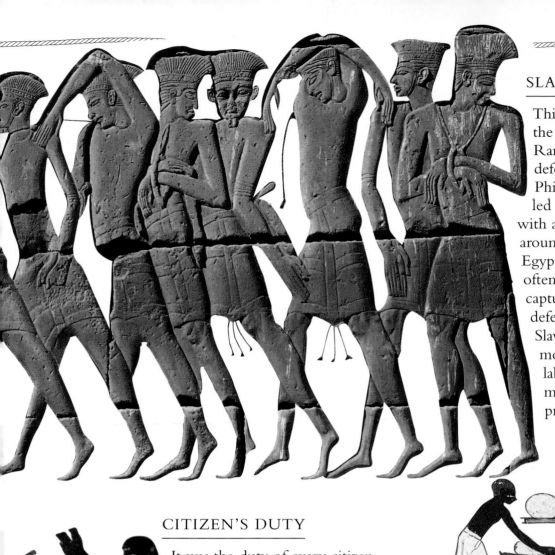

SLAVE TRADE

This relief from the temple of Rameses III shows defeated Philistines being led into captivity with a rope tied around their necks. Egyptian society often used slaves captured from defeated countries. Slaves provided most of the labour for the massive building programmes.

CITIZEN'S DUTY

It was the duty of every citizen to prevent crimes or to punish criminals. If witnesses did not do their duty, they were beaten with branches.

LAW OF DECLARATION

Each year every adult had to provide a written report to their local magistrate stating how they made their living. If they did not, it was assumed they were criminals and they were executed.

HONOUR AMONG THIEVES

Among other things, Thoth was the god of wisdom and truth. Here, in baboon form, he is catching a thief. People could actually register as thieves and declare their earnings. However, if a victim could describe what was stolen from him, he could claim 75 percent back, but the thief kept the rest!

TRANSPORT AND SCIENCE

The ancient Egyptians introduced and developed many new ideas and inventions. Because Egypt was very dry, there were few trees and therefore little wood for building and other purposes. The Egyptians used stone and papyrus to make many things. Papyrus is a triangular-stemmed reed that grows to about three metres tall. Most settlements were near the banks of the River Nile so the easiest way to travel, especially for long journeys, was by boat. Egyptian boats were not that good on the open sea, but they could cope with the calmer waters of the Nile.

PALANQUIN

The Pharaohs travelled in a chariot or a decorated carriage for long journeys. For short journeys, they would be carried in a palanquin – a canopied chair.

CREATING A CALENDAR

Egyptian priests were also astronomers. By studying the movements of heavenly bodies they were able to accurately predict various natural events. They invented an annual calendar of 365 days, divided into 12 equal months of 30 days, followed by five 'complementary' days.

WHEELED VEHICLES

In about 3000 BCE, it is thought that the Sumerians created the first wheeled vehicle. The idea was copied and developed by the Egyptians, who made many more sophisticated vehicles, though none survive.

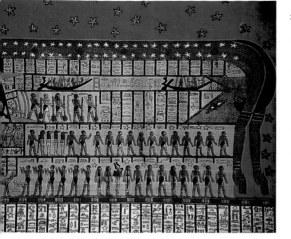

THE SKY GOD

The Egyptians studied the heavens in great detail and formed a theory about how the universe began. They saw the early chaos of the universe as water (Nun). The sun god Atum came out of the sea as land (as Egypt itself did from the annual flood). From this came air (Shu), moisture (Tefnut), earth (Geb) and sky (Nut).

REED BOATS

Many of the boats used in ancient Egypt were not made of wood, which was expensive and difficult to obtain, but of papyrus. The reeds were tightly bundled and then strapped to a frame, rather like roof thatching. They were made waterproof by tying several layers together.

WRITING IT ALL DOWN

Flat strips of papyrus were used in layers to form a smooth and long-lasting paper. This was cut into lengths and rolled into scrolls. Even the pens were made from papyrus stems.

RIVER TRANSPORT

This model, found in a tomb, is probably typical of many of the boats that sailed the Nile. It was powered by oars and a small sail, and steered with a large oar at the stern (back), like a rudder.

THOTH

Thoth, the god of the moon, was the divine intelligence of the universe. He taught humans language, writing, art, music, architecture and mathematics. He was often represented by Ibis, a bird with a curved beak.

ANUBIS

Anubis, the god of mummification, was represented by a jackal. Jackals often visited cemeteries, probably to eat corpses but they were seen as protectors of the dead. The priest shown here is wearing a jackal mask.

THE SPHINX

Standing at Giza by the pyramids is a sphinx (half-man, half-lion). Carved from solid rock in about 2500 BCE, it is 35.6 metres long and 15.5 metres high.

CULT OF THE DEAD

To the ancient Egyptians, death was seen simply as a short stage between this life and the afterlife. Bodies were preserved by mummification. Books of the dead were buried with the bodies to help ensure safe passage to the next life.

RELIGION

THE TEMPLE OF KARNAK

The columns and walls from the temple at Karnak (above) are decorated with lotus and papyrus carvings. The temple was dedicated to Amun-Re, protector of the pharaohs. Amun-Re is a combination of Amun (which means 'hidden') and Re (the sun god).

There were several hundred different gods and goddesses in ancient Egypt, many of whom lived as animals on Earth. When priests carried out their rituals, they would often wear an animal mask, to give the impression that they were the actual god. It is hard to understand the Egyptian gods, especially as the same animal might represent several different gods in different regions. However, the one 'true god', and king of all the other gods, was Amun-Re, the sun god. The ancient Egyptians kept many libraries, mostly of sacred writings, and many talk of a belief in an afterlife. They believed in an underworld, called Duat, where the dead had to make a dangerous journey to reach a kind of 'promised land'.

THE SACRED TRIAD

Amun-Re was seen as a triad (group of three) of gods and goddess, Amun (the father), Mouth (the mother) and Khons (the son).

ISIS

This picture shows the goddess Isis, suckling her infant son, Horus. Isis and Osiris were told by Thoth to make humans behave better. Isis was a fertility goddess, linked to mother Earth and the cycle of birth, death and rebirth in the afterlife. Her shrines in temples were often looked after by women.

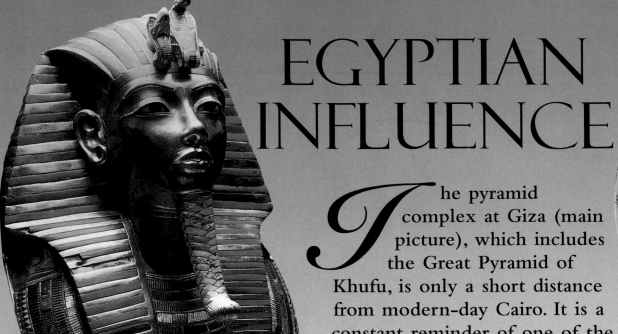

EGYPTIAN INFLUENCE

*T*he pyramid complex at Giza (main picture), which includes the Great Pyramid of Khufu, is only a short distance from modern-day Cairo. It is a constant reminder of one of the greatest civilizations of the ancient world. Ancient Egypt is not the oldest civilization known (although it was once thought to be) but it has left a lasting impression, especially its architecture and style of art. It is also thought that it was the Egyptians who came up with the unit of time known as a 'week'. They named the seven days of the week after the five known planets – Mars, Mercury, Jupiter, Venus and Saturn – and the sun and the moon.

TUTANKHAMUN'S TREASURE

King Tutankhamun lived during the 18th dynasty and died around the age of 18 in c.1344 BCE. When his tomb was opened in 1922, it was the only tomb of a pharaoh, so far discovered, to have survived intact. Inside was an astonishing collection of jewellery, artefacts and artwork. His magnificent face mask, shown above, was made of gold, inlaid with blue lapis lazuli. Treasures from the tomb have been displayed around the world, and the exhibition in Cairo Museum is now a major tourist attraction.